LISTENING FOR WINTER

KARTHIK BLKN

Copyright © Karthik Blkn
All Rights Reserved.

ISBN 979-888546011-8

This book has been published with all efforts taken to make the material error-free after the consent of the author. However, the author and the publisher do not assume and hereby disclaim any liability to any party for any loss, damage, or disruption caused by errors or omissions, whether such errors or omissions result from negligence, accident, or any other cause.

While every effort has been made to avoid any mistake or omission, this publication is being sold on the condition and understanding that neither the author nor the publishers or printers would be liable in any manner to any person by reason of any mistake or omission in this publication or for any action taken or omitted to be taken or advice rendered or accepted on the basis of this work. For any defect in printing or binding the publishers will be liable only to replace the defective copy by another copy of this work then available.

For my family, and the gods

Contents

Acknowledgements *vii*

1. In Primordium 1
2. Experientia And The Spirit 3
3. Tears In Levity 6
4. Mirth And Rendition 9
5. Ego Of Indulgence 13
6. The Infant, The Sow 16
7. Of Erratic Inceptions And The Abstract Idea 19
8. The Unravelling 23
9. Vanity In Old Memory 25
10. Death, Of The Second State 28
11. Through The Ages 31

Contents

Acknowledgements

First and foremost, I want to express my endless love and gratitude to my parents, who have always supported my many dreams, who have inspired and encouraged me to write and get my work out into the world, and who have been my constant support. To my sister, my dearest friend, who spent countless hours editing this book and patiently put up with my many eccentricities and tantrums, thank you.

Special thanks to my English Teacher in school, Mr. Winston Gardner, who, with his invaluable inputs and encouragement, always pushed me to write better poetry.

To my friends, who have come and gone over the years, but have ever encouraged my writing with kind words, especially when I needed them most, thank you.

This book owes its existence to the cosmic teacher, for being the fire of creation that stitched all the countless strings of inspiration and thought together in the writing of these poems.

And thank you, dear reader, for picking up my book! I really do hope you enjoy reading these poems!

1. IN PRIMORDIUM

Give little thought to bleak meanderings
of the vessel of this immense present.
Realize in this self the infinitely able,
meditate upon the summation of material futures,
in the realization of their temporal designs.
Find unbridled awe in a vast expanse,
in a realm of unfettered multitudes,
of new reality couched and taking form
in the void crevices of existence.

Graze the azure plains of primordial inception.
Become washed in pristine streams of knowing.
Drink of waters of profoundest depth;
uncover in their bounty the seeds of wisdom.
Here, neither time nor elemental rumblings
truncate the relish of moments that reverberate
through the emancipated peaks of mind.

The inequitable grime of these somber realities
bleed the senses ignorant of a yearning
for transcendental bonds and learning
that we are finite dreamlings to a slumbering god-
corporeal shadows of the eternally curious.

In time, these abstractions shall cease to exist.
That ignorance purged in the forges of the pall,
the boundless mind unbound of gathered doom
shall become divine in the ether of bliss.

2. EXPERIENTIA AND THE SPIRIT

Salutations do we humbly take
to the sovereign of this studied space!
Whose myriad eyes rest their weight,
upon a pristine celestial state;
constant purveyor of the threads of fate,
extant monuments to thy determined grace.

From amongst the putrid plenty,
merciful shroud doth us ferry
to burgeoning peaks and shimmering waters.
From the teeth of myriad machinations
that rendered this form too-
of the myriad in thy memory-
among the forgetful suffering,
to be destined for the dying.
Embittered imperfects in another time
to be forgotten at once in this sublime.

For what glory is carried from our dwellings?
What learnings from servile earnings
that, like tenants, we are not to keep?
To see to only lose memory

of all learning, imbued in vacant waters,
lost to us in fiery altars.

Primacy to thee in our seeking in
the tree of mutating climes.
In the tribute, we bring to present, is
seamless bounty to bless ethereal mines.
Of material happenings that grazed the mind,
grand sayings and spent ages, parables
in countless other worlds imbibed
come to be realized in numerous lives.

Our transient paths are for thine appetites
to secure treasure for an endless stock.
Myriad moments to award thee
among Neptune's infinite flock.
That voyage we make, now in toil,
to moments in perpetual turmoil,
we seek the breaking of the wave
to only be foiled in its trifles.

We may take no memory of these presents
but we may yet remember,
as minute Piscean beings
of the multitudinous sea
that have the god's many locks to bear.
That, though lost in starved pursuit,

We must remain ever mindful of the vast bosom
that sustains our being there.

Wistful moaning breaks the calm
to call us forth to new lodgings.
We sail unto the horizon for great gatherings
to bring refill for thy yearnings.
Beckoning shall this transit land
in a sojourn of shifting sands.

For the resolute end to all solitary wails,
to the wars that are raging in tired seas
in the rise of timeless tides,
these parlays are but too brief.

3. TEARS IN LEVITY

What dolor keeps your heart?
That perennial levity that lines your notes
permutes into feeble moaning of sorrow,
skin folds doused in screeching tones.

What nature eats at your visage
of dolor garbed in ebullience?
Your tears are evidenced by arid ways,
that form gray shadows in the pale,
that meander down your sunken face
to the unembellished remnants of age.
The parched drought lines on your face
speak of sincerest art and drowning heart;
this great machine must rumble all the same.

Lithe movements speak not of the weight they bear,
all ever subsumed in the delicacy of your gait,
set to symphonies that do relentless pursuers make.

These melancholic vessels do look upon you,
as him upon whom nature's lighter vestiges
are so lavished, though forfeit of their own.
And, distinguished appetites are delirious yet,

for him in whose distractions are their labours met:
the grumbling beast whose aspiration
casts a shadow that dwarfs itself.
In whose gyrations their beaten flesh is livened,
whose cacophony embroiders their attentions,
whose myriad movements their ovations leech,
into whose solitary recesses he poured intrigue,
reflections reposed in uncharted minds, the crowd
in whose leering eyes are countless mirrors cast.

The ubiquitous gaze of varied vice,
transmuted minds whose machinations
were on a singular thing transfixed.
The promiscuous organs of their eyes
differently engaged, all rapture bound-
distinct manifestations with the same catalyst.

The varied essence that would possess your face,
tall legends to animate your stage,
of man's banalities and triumphs, both,
grandiose tales you willingly gave.

The gyrations here are now of shriller form
brought on by unattended repetition;
uninspired derivations shorn of grace.
Reverberations that sting memory.

Alas, another form shall fill that stage,
these halls betrothed to another face,
We commend your form to mindless hearts,
and your tale to a bygone age!

For one autumn eve it was that day
when all did flock to glean
the tidings that you brought for all,
though momentarily veiled by seams.
For the strands that you wove upon
the stage you chose to bear your pall,
and deathlike loom aloft the hall
that mourns you in its call.

4. MIRTH AND RENDITION

There is no mirth in rendition,
orphaned child of departed life
whose minstrels do stare us hence.
Gleeful artisan that wrought
this realm in ink and time,
letters doused in inspired grandeur
bound eternally to immutable parchment.

An aborted epic, in this grand canvas.
Tapestry, these eyes shall never witness,
of more than longing and unrest,
immense possibilities were intended.
These tales were meant never
for tired retellings of banal themes;
that these spaces bereft of narration,
have now slated in their passage
little variance in an infinite scheme.

The occupants absent completion
do implore gleaning eyes for meaning,
and speak to us an oft repeated tale
of longing for closure, and aborted endings.

For absent addition, this tale differs
only in cast and milieu
dredged upon this ill-fated canvas,
for this unfinished realm awaits
the absent poet that drew these spring letters
that float, unmindful of their fate, towards some end.
They covet what change they shall not be sent,
to lay desolate there, awaiting creation-
their creator's indulgent striation-
as the first beings that waited,
for this god that retired for rest,
but rest for his toil, was ebb for theirs
that are eternally forlorn in his passing.

Only conjuring eyes shall gather
there are no tides or tempests there,
nor winter blizzard or summer air,
no sudden ills might befall it,
no momentous joys to visit
save the renditions of suffered tragedies,
and the touch of cherished memories
far removed from natural shuffling.
Constancy is the tragedy that ails it;
these words have little weight in moored minds.

The erudite keepers of all vision
that require stricture in all production,

that judge to have erasure of imperfection,
will seek its redoing in changed worlds,
its removal from its own natures,
that give no pause for appreciation
for fate's intended conclusion.

Abounding age shall reveal all leanings
that meaning revision may seldom confer;
all things unfold to find in time their seat,
for time and eternity may never meet.

This stifled tale shall bleed into myriad minds.
What his hand shall nevermore guide
their mindful workings might revive
to see the shifts that shall come upon
this fabled autumn realm;
its tired occupants do abide.
That garden unabated awaits
any willing breath of creation.

What joy to have known the occupants!
To have felt their words, upon his lips,
to have known them more
than they might know themselves.
To have read their illustrious myths,
to have seen them grown in the slate of his being,
in stoked embers of creation.

This portion shall fan cinders of envy
to now only ever be read
with the waning finality of your artistry,
far removed from your lofty intending;
words and occupants shall cease to matter.
The abrupt stifling of your hurried tale
shall suffice for prying minds.
The occupants here shall eternally seek
to find their quietude in impassioned eyes.

5. EGO OF INDULGENCE

Ego suckles from indulgent breasts;
petulant babe that clings
firm around her troubled chest,
her mind shall savor no rest.
Indignant orifices give succor
to ravenous appetites for nourishment's sake,
gives will to a want for incessant satiation-
the dawn of lavish wants
and nurture to ruinous tastes.

Only It can tell her from the crowd,
marked to all by Its many charms,
It must always be close,
ever in her doting arms.
The crude thing that cares not for reason
wails, court ardent willing eyes.
From the indifferent, It shall seek attention
and the provision of constant pleasing
to surmise material happenings, as It knows best,
to be lauded, in every moment passing.

It grips tight around her neck,

the suffocation brings comfort
to her, necessary is Its righteous avengement,
for Its hurt must be her battle drum,
until her bosom is sore, battered,
for neither tremors, nor the past, shall humble it,
only the strain of passing years,
the accumulating maim of the sun and rain,
shall ever tame It.
It, like all persuasions, deserves time
and the weight of compounding years,
but unbridled, she is to stay this course,
until needling age shall sap Its tears.

In their slumber she awaits a moment's peace,
but It is her petulant companion,
ever restless, seldom at ease.
To cradle Its pertinent girth
is her accumulated fate.
For Its mighty weight
the earth has no fit seat.

It must have a moment to walk,
touch the hard earth under Its feet.
From above, when it shall arrive
It shall momentarily find
her feet firm upon the ground.
No immediate tempest needs braving,

nor pride shall seek Its saving.
There is firm earth beneath her feet,
It can find comfort in their certain gait,
restive passion expended in their motion.

That absent the sting of Its thrall,
the brutal sway of Its afflicted being,
her alleviated mind shall come to find
a moment of calm in the transient storm
that brings the barrage of insulted indignation
to give ease to the better persuasions of her being;
to brave the storms from without her walls and
within she shall find temperate winds
astride the approaching dawn.
Her will shall temper Its hold, in time,
to brave the blast of graver storms.

6. THE INFANT, THE SOW

The weary sun breathed warm upon the Fair.
The throng perspired of a boisterous bustle.
A pregnant creature, of dubious note,
did steal a glimpse, a whisper there,
as she sauntered, in uncertainty,
making her way, to a sty, in disrepair.

There was none that there did listen,
no leering eyes that gave audience,
no tongue to spin threads of scandal,
save for the solemn sow that suckled her litter.

Cruelest agony was to come uninvited.
She roiled uninterrupted in her torment,
her wails choked by fear of greater pains
to be suffered from outward maiming.
The moment drew on like a timeless terror,
she heaved to release with all she could conjure,
until all at once, a soiled, minute thing emerged
to fall to the straw and dirt that did gather.

Eager babe of meager womb,

expectant of infancy's fresh joys.
O, where the fates have cast thee!
By what jealous old god cursed
to be cast among piles of excrement;
the scent of indifference that corrupts
and clouds thy virgin vision,
the grunting of the nurturing sow,
the first lullaby, these ears shall ever hear.

None have seen this pittance in thy birth,
obligated upon this desolate soul,
that womb not given willingly
seeks to be rid of thy reeking flesh.

Her vision mustn't meet its frail form
lest her heart be moved to stay.
But youthful foibles make it felt
that impending troubles are potent,
great injustices that she must comprehend,
and this babe that lays so still has met
the unsavory end of suffering.

The knot of primordial nurture dislodged
the flesh vestige of their filial bond.
She staggers away, makes to a solemn bath,
where ritual waters shall carry this past.

What care our minds, if thee be dying?
Thy flooded canals shall forever hear
garbled words, and muffled missives,
decay's somber humming tunes;
accrued sin purged in potent fumes.

But wailing disturbs the frolic of wallowing piglets,
erupts from the fragile infant therein lying.
But there is none that gives hear
in the mutiny of the bustling scales-
until its waning pleadings pierce a willing ear,
hands come to see her wrapped in luxuriant rags.
She departs to saner or crueler tomorrows,
the thoroughfare sings of commerce and hope.
Her cries shall fade in time,
to be drowned in the Fair's forebodings.

7. OF ERRATIC INCEPTIONS AND THE ABSTRACT IDEA

'Tis my name they call,
echoes off the empty hall,
I like its sound, the ring withal,
and soon I shall know its end.

To what convention, to what place,
I have no wind of such,
ambiguity shrouds the pursuit's face,
as do the depths I touch.
Something brews, I tell it true,
inception of some kind,
reveling, perhaps, of profounder note,
such things appall the mind.
Dubious things such matters are
I think to only think,
that thinking tires, I am tired-
tis noon, to slumber I sink.

'Tis evening, I am exuberant!
Unlike the sullenness of such,

'Tis a rarity for such as me,
foreboding that is kind.
And then I think luxuriant still
that if such eve be full of mirth,
can other days and other times
not be so benign?

To what end do I now proceed,
and where tread to now;
to what belief still endearing,
I forget, but here am come.
I tread on miry roads and marsh
and still its meaning eludes.
Without relent I follow sense,
as do I this quaint pursuit.
A weary day, so this has been,
myriad moments refresh my stock,
for there's much I've said and much I've seen-
'tis midnight on the clock.

My sense reels as the fantasy slides,
Gargantuan forms surround me.
Their words bid my sense abide,
as I comprehend all I see.
It was something we'd done,
they relate to me now,
a match of guile, we'd had.

If that be true,
then tell I pray,
my fibs- how good were they?
They would not speak,
much like the lifeless
toys that never told.
But of what
transpired here,
remembrance has not awoke.

They recount I was a cogent fibber,
though no joust was won.
Do I smirk in subtle rancor,
or scowl at its very sound?
Or sit as I do now calm, composed,
and hurt as is my way?
Or relish it rather as some distinct,
erudition that greets this day?

Does this learning then conduct our being?
These manifold shots of grace-
the portion we are meting out-
the entirety we stand to face.
My spirit grazed by such sensation,
I perceive in humanness again,
that longing is good, and desperation,
when such we stand to gain.

And in that thought I know for sure,
that artless, singular thing.
I hear my name, I like its sound,
and now I know its end.

8. THE UNRAVELLING

This unravelling edifice awaits resolution:
solemn walkways and naked keeps
bereft of stirring, have etched this cessation.
In the pages of all recorded things
this too shall be commended to drab writings,
uncommitted recordings its solitary testaments.
These tenements rupture under their malice,
of grave wrongs that wore moral garb,
like glaciers have waited beyond its gaze,
to disperse and run in icy river ways
in the summer when the watchful have left.
Ablution, rites for the departed dead.

It breathes heavy through the malodorous air
that ventilates its hollow holdings,
that chokes her failing lungs,
to spew maladies from sundry addled vents
to great mouths of large appetites;
of littered veins and putrid drains,
withered sinews shall fail it hence.
In the time, when all doings are forgotten
for the ends of a greater beyond,
to offer great words, with paltry fervour,

that cannot save, what they cannot stir.

Reminisce upon thine glory days,
exalted names and crowded ways.
These accruing lines temper thine tread.
Arms, these, but brittle recompense
thy instruments, that in old bade,
the earth beneath their feet astir,
now a vestige- brittle instrument,
ostentation does their reason become:
grey figurines upon thine tenements
quiver beneath thy wilted brow.

Age shall meet this grandeur in its turn,
when all its laden children have left.
To ash and dust shall its pillars burn,
to fade in solemn river beds.

9. VANITY IN OLD MEMORY

There are no fruits in vanity.
Mortal titles do not rattle the walls
of storied halls. The invocation
of thy name doth not evoke humility.
Thy kinship bringeth no elation,
haloed deeds provoke no ovation,
in the minds of these, mere mortal, things.

This realm remembers you now
as it does all the divinely parted.
And time shall unleash its carrion eaters
to pick at your naked bones through the ages,
to only take what men most desire:
the securement of their own cause.
To the vain now departed-
I shall hear of you only in passing.

If you could only see the putrid tongue
that bears your holy name-
to what purpose employed-
among what squalid company cast-
far removed from whence it stood,

long after you shall have passed.

Faithless gems adorn simpler forms.
Your crown sits heavy upon another;
the dirt gives less than it shall reclaim.
For what do luxuries matter
to dwellers of depleting frame,
their purpose to secure for other tenants
the matter for their sustenance.
Save the coins that shall remain
the weights upon your vacant vision.
Neither you nor body shall preserve
what cannot be its to retain.

Of trinkets of truth, and lies in large,
of purchased accolades, and terrible tidings,
equivocation shall pour doubly forth.
And unsheathed fangs shall draw their due
of false words and misled minds, both,
they shall consume in full, of you.

These myths and recorded rumors
do honour to your gloried being;
find curation in obscure scrolls,
to only be read in expedience.
Or, be so far removed from abject truths,
they may in time, be dust with you.

Revelation haunts your bitter presents,
the chasm from whence you observe
this humble state that remains-
that prospers- in your absence.
You shall now truly comprehend
there are no rectifications that can be made,
nor conciliatory words to be said,
and that grace has no name
that is in vacant palms to expend.

10. DEATH, OF THE SECOND STATE

Astral watcher of the ephemeral pasture
that peers through the waking glass.
Famished eater of life's bile and nectar,
lamp holder to the uncharted path.
We ask leave to board your craft
where gravest debts are met
with dispassionate settlement.
Chaperone for the ghastly new born,
render us to shores of dreamless sand,
where remembrance of yonder shan't haunt,
the auroral glimmers of an epoch past
belie the freeing shadows of eternity.

We bring no aurum trinkets for the ferry
for the boatman that rests upon its mast,
nor treasures of old do we carry.
We bring but the travails of a sordid past,
the momentary pleasures that were summarily lost-
we have only this to offer to thee.
For perilous is the way across the opaque sea
unblinking eyes that stare through black waters.
There is no need here for hope,

nor bitter mead nor redeeming smoke;
the ferry will rest us in pale shawls,
journeys to awake in grand or grim halls.

There are no choirs here
nor fatal singing or chanting for company,
no paeans ever read, nor grandiose epitaphs
will ever calm the waking dead-
only the looming rhythm of laughter,
that haunts this gloomy ever after.

Commute us to lands of untold moons,
of seasons quick of change.
Deliverer from corporeal pangs,
eternal bane to mortal pain.

Were we but a chasm in your colossal memory,
as bits lost in cosmic paradox
never to find your company,
until all that remains is strife
for timely dispersion of servient life!

But we remain all in gratitude to thee.
All, ever at your grim mercy,
ever wary of your call,
that quiet to beckon all
to timeless realms beyond the ash,

to the void stomach of all happening.
Uncertain angst shall ever mar
our sojourn in this boundless vast.

11. THROUGH THE AGES

These ceaseless wheels turn to make our way,
to great nothings where new matter springs,
to the unfurled potentials of this material cosmos,
to unstirring waters, the promise of life we bring.

For I am the wheel of countless worlds,
incubator of the seeds of their birth.
For I traverse the fields of the unrealized
that come to be nurtured in my tender stride.

The solemn wheels must endure,
for where their tread marks the naked land
no trembling feet may go.
We are the bringer and remover of eternal vice,
revealer of unladen multitudes,
venerated by the hum of promethean storms,
star paladins to keep my eternal ways.

These cold hands shall permeate all,
to be never touched by their warmth.
But all shall ever feel
my fleeing cloak upon their brow,

no eyes to observe and minds to follow
to the crude beginnings and esoteric ends of things.

Of melancholy and mirth, I have heard-
melodies that stir remembrance.
That past that I shall neither take nor keep,
of these presents, neither you nor memory.

Of great telling birthed of dubious tongues,
of the wealthy fall, and the trodden in their trappings,
sages born of the unscrupulous young,
vitriol spawned of the outwardly sane.
These tales made and remade,
myriad renderings, as stories told anew,
I have tasted the hollow climax of every myth,
that hides in the recesses of beating hearts.

All beings become transmuted in us,
all things brought to mind from dust.
This mighty march is humbled in our path,
beneath this churning, the oceans part.

My will to blunt the sharpest blade,
the precious to lose all luster in my way,
I maim the tall edifice,
to recast in higher form.
From them to lift all beings

we become the eternal wind,
that gallops with the living.

I shall have no remembrance
of these myriad instances
for these wheels hold
the mass of all material beings.
They shall never stutter or stall,
for somber reminisces of experienced things.

Have I no excess to gift from this chest
to these that ask for more,
nor meanderings or deviation can I affect
in my eternal passage that is etched,
written in the vast minutiae of existence,
whose countless cells look to us for direction.

These piquant eyes now are weary.
Much have their sights observed
in voyages that span the infinite dreamscape,
unwashed by the gush of tears.
Unrested, they shall preserve
the travails of accumulating years,
for such I have beheld
in existence's shifting scales.
Alas! There is more to be told;
I course the infernal realm of dying suns-

an eternity remains, to unfold.

9 798885 460118

Printed by Libri Plureos GmbH in Hamburg,
Germany